The Zoo Olympics

The people came to see the Zoo Olympic Games. They clapped when the animals came out.

The gazelle won the running race and got a gold medal.
"Gazelles can run very fast," said the people.

The kangaroo won the high jump.
She got a gold medal, too.
"Kangaroos are good at jumping,"
said the people.

The sea lion won the swimming race.
The people clapped when the sea lion got a gold medal.
"Sea lions are good at swimming," said the people.

The hippopotamus got a gold medal for winning the tug of war.
Hippopotamuses are very strong.
"Well done, Hippopotamus!" the people shouted.

The elephant got a gold medal
for weight-lifting and the people
clapped and clapped.
"Elephants are good at weight-lifting,"
said the people.

The story of the Zoo Olympics was in the newspaper, but the story was wrong.

It said that the gazelle
won the swimming race.

It said that the kangaroo won the tug of war.

The newspaper story said that the sea lion won the weight-lifting.

It said that the hippopotamus won the running race.

It said that the elephant got a gold medal for the high jump.

The people laughed and laughed at the story.
"This story will not win a gold medal," they said. "This story is all wrong!"